REFLECTIONS

Reflections

A BOOK OF INSPIRING QUOTES, AND THOUGHTS TO HELP BUILD **CONFIDENCE**, AND **SELF-ESTEEM**.

EUGENE NAPOLEON

REFLECTIONS
A BOOK OF INSPIRING QUOTES, AND THOUGHTS TO
HELP BUILD CONFIDENCE, AND SELF-ESTEEM.

Copyright © 2020 Eugene Napoleon.

All rights reserved. No part of this book may be used or reproduced by any means, graphic, electronic, or mechanical, including photocopying, recording, taping or by any information storage retrieval system without the written permission of the author except in the case of brief quotations embodied in critical articles and reviews.

iUniverse books may be ordered through booksellers or by contacting:

iUniverse
1663 Liberty Drive
Bloomington, IN 47403
www.iuniverse.com
1-800-Authors (1-800-288-4677)

Because of the dynamic nature of the Internet, any web addresses or links contained in this book may have changed since publication and may no longer be valid. The views expressed in this work are solely those of the author and do not necessarily reflect the views of the publisher, and the publisher hereby disclaims any responsibility for them.

Any people depicted in stock imagery provided by Getty Images are models, and such images are being used for illustrative purposes only. Certain stock imagery © Getty Images.

ISBN: 978-1-5320-9155-1 (sc)
ISBN: 978-1-5320-9156-8 (e)

Library of Congress Control Number: 2020900359

Print information available on the last page.

iUniverse rev. date: 01/14/2020

Dedication

"I am grateful to God, family, and friends for helping me to evolve into the man I am today. It takes many hands of support to build anything of value. I am thankful to all of those individuals that had a hand in helping me on my journey."

"To my beloved mother, and father, thank you for blessing me with unconditional love. My mother taught me the importance of being a good human being, and being a man of character, with morals. She gave me a strong foundation to stand on, and I am her legacy."

"To my loving wife Tracey, you are my rock, my soulmate, my everything. Thank you for the tremendous love, and support that you provide. You are a wonderful wife, and mother. I am grateful to God for blessing our union. I love you more than words can say."

"To my son Brandon, I am blessed by God to be your father. You are my greatest accomplishment. As I watch your journey, I am proud of your steps as you walk towards your personal growth. My love for you is beyond measure. I love you to the moon, and back."

CHAPTER 1
LOVE / RELATIONSHIPS: 10 QUOTES

"Allow the love in your heart to speak louder than your words."

"Your eyes will always speak the truth when it comes to matters of the heart."

"When you love, and respect yourself, others will start to take notice."

"Relationships are built on trust, so walk in your own truth."

"The reflections you want others to
see starts with honesty."

"Love, not hatred changes things!"

"Be the shining light in a heart filled with darkness."

"Relationships are like roads, they have twists, turns, highs, and lows, but you determine the final destination."

"Be faithful in your efforts, patient in your approach, and steady in your intentions."

"Loyalty, and trust are key building blocks in any relationship."

Chapter 2

MAKING BETTER DECISIONS: 10 QUOTES

"It's your life, and your choices, so don't listen to anyone that has poor intentions."

"If you always think first, your second thought,
and actions should reflect that."

"Personal character, morals, and values, should be the foundation of your decisions."

"If you want to change the narrative, you need to rewrite the script of your choices."

"Stand strong in the face of adversity, and stand on your own convictions."

"Do what you're supposed to do, not what you want to do!"

"Taking responsibility is one part of personal growth."

"Don't allow negative energy to drive your decisions."

"Don't allow someone else's issues to become your issues."

"Your future success will depend on
the choices you make today."

Chapter 3
EMOTIONS: 10 QUOTES

"Allow passion to drive you, but not destroy you."

"Don't allow anger to define you."

"It takes a strong person to sometimes show weakness."

"Anger is a state of mind, not a condition."

"Don't allow someone else to control your
emotions, thoughts, and actions."

"What's important to you, may not be important to others. So manage your feelings."

"The eyes speak what the mouth
finds most difficult to say."

"Don't allow the stress of nonverbal communication to create a toxic environment."

"Learn to listen to your heart, it speaks the truth."

"Don't allow painful thoughts to become your reality."

Chapter 4

SPORTS / MOTIVATION: 10 QUOTES

"It takes one step at a time to start the process of walking towards your dreams."

"I take from my past to inspire my future."

"Be disciplined, driven, focused, and success will follow."

"Your success will be determined by the hours you put in working towards your goals."

"Success is the completion of a task."

"Cherish consistency, it will open doors that were once locked."

"Spiritual development is the foundation for overall lifelong success, and happiness."

"Believe in yourself! The X-factor
starts, and ends with you."

"Be driven by a burning desire, and a plan to be successful, not just by words."

"NO WORDS just ACTION!"

Chapter 5
THOUGHTS: 10 QUOTES

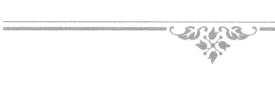

"You cannot invite everyone to sit at the table, be selective."

"Be the version of yourself that you want to see in others."

"See what you want, know what you
want, now go get what you want!"

"Exercise patience, and understanding.
Anything broken can be fixed."

"Execution starts with preparation."

"Just, because you have eyes, does not mean you see things clearly."

"Stop taking things for granted. Be smart, and learn from the benefits of past experiences."

"Be aware of the fact, that not everyone wants you to succeed."

"It takes organizational skills to prepare a solid blueprint for future success."

"You must dream real, dream big, and dream often. Your success is up to you!"

CPSIA information can be obtained
at www.ICGtesting.com
Printed in the USA
BVHW070557090322
630905BV00001B/99